CONFESSIONS OF A PREACHER'S KID

By Alfie March

COPYWRITE & DISCLAIMER

Copyright © 2021 by Alfie March /Nixie Press
Cover & Interior Design © 2021 Ania Halama
aniahalama.com

IBSN 978-1-7367893-1-5
Library of Congress Control Number: 2021914730

All rights reserved. No part of this book may be reproduced or used in any manner without written permission of the copyright owner except for the use of quotations in a book review. Copyright protects freedom of speech and artistic expression. It promotes diversity and the united human desire to overcome struggle through creation.
For more information, e-mail: prosperitygrapes@gmail.com

Title: Confessions of a Preacher's Kid: Self-actualization Poetry

Subjects: Poetry, Coming-Of-Age, Self-Actualization, Spiritual Discovery, Self-Help Poetry, Revelation, Coping, Burn-Out, Growing Up In Ministry/Christianity, Identity

FIRST EDITION

https://www.authoralfiemarch.com

TABLE OF CONTENTS

FORWARD 5

CHAPTER ONE: LOW VIBRATIONS

We Cannot Help But Judge	7
Is It Worth It?	8
Different Me	9
Where Do I Belong?	10
Ok With It	11
Not Like You	12
Alone	13
Cancel It	14
Deceived	15
Got Away	16
I Am Drowning	17
No One Forgets	18
The Prophet	19
A Fall From Grace	20
Cheater	21
Same Saga	22
Descending	23
What We Don't Know	24

CHAPTER TWO: SPIRITUAL INTIMACY

Your Love	27
Our Place	28
Only You	29
Who You Are To Me	30
Song: I Will Wait	31
Self Worth	32
You Taught Me	33
Holding Hands	34
Memories	35
Starting Over	36

The Room	37
He Understands	38

CHAPTER THREE: BACKSLIDING

Backsliding	41
Where Is The Promise?	42
Thank You	43
Happy	44
Truths	45
Misunderstanding	46
They Know I Am A Fake	47
Who Am I?	48
Yesterday's Prayer	49
Mirror	50
I Wish I Never Went	51
Loneliness	52
Unfortunate	53

CHAPTER FOUR: YOU, ME & THINGS FORESEEN

Retrospect	55
A Fleeting Prayer	56
Learning Fast	57
My Best Friend Melissa	58
Worst Thoughts	59
Me	60
Breaking Up	61
Dear Future Children	62
Advice	63
Leaving	64
How You Turned Out	65

CHAPTER FIVE: CHURCH SPLITS AND OFFENSE

Help Me To Remember, Help Me To Forget	67
Truth	68
Struggle	69
I Hate You For This	70

Smothering	*71*
Gone	*72*
You Waited Too Long	*73*

CHAPTER SIX: THE ONE

Preparation	*75*
Two Steps Back	*76*
Unbroken Dreams	*77*
When You Let It Go	*78*
The Perfect One	*79*
My Favorite Prayer	*80*

CHAPTER SEVEN: THE END

Here To Stay	*83*
Epiphany	*84*
Bitterness	*85*
Lost Sheep	*86*
Priceless Love	*87*
Wits End	*88*
The Least Of These	*89*
Answered Prayer	*90*
Shalom	*91*

FORWARD

Growing up as a pastor's kid is a different life. At an early age, I wrestled with my spiritual identity comparative to my physical existence. I was lonely, and a deep thinker. I felt a lot of pressure on many different levels. Naturally, in my environment, I developed many core beliefs over the years. Some, I am still trying to unload, such as: I cannot make mistakes without messing everything up for everyone who depends on me, I need other people's permission to have expensive things, and feelings are always misleading - telling the truth leads to terrible offenses.

As I evaluated the lives around me, I determined that life is meant to be hard. People are either takers or givers. Embarking on your own journey is unnecessary. Be obedient and save yourself the trouble of your own faith journey. What you want is not important if it will upset someone. These are all examples of affirmations I adopted as a child. While I blame no one, I have realized the detriment of some of these subconscious beliefs.

Everyone's journey is unique. This is the evolution of an immature mind, heart, and soul. I am releasing many of the burdens and celebrating some of the beauty of my life as a preacher's kid. God has proved faithful through it all. I hope the highs and lows of my young journey are evident in the prose.

Honesty has led me to the most profound self-discovery, that I must make a demand for peace and abundance to flow into my life. At one time, depression, failure, and chronic illness seemed to be my default state. It has taken relentless pursuit of faith and a huge conscious effort to overcome them. These poems were all written between twelve and twenty-two years of age. I am living and breathing to be real about my journey and to be an overcomer in the flesh. You have a story to tell, and so do I. I pray that you find something of substance for your time.

CHAPTER ONE
LOW VIBRATIONS

WE CANNOT HELP BUT JUDGE

I say something or nothing
Their opinions percolate
There is always an inner hope that I will be accepted
Mostly rejected
They look away or gawk
I wear the judgements that boldly dress my life

Very black
Very white
Is how I would describe my surroundings
Others often turn their head in disinterest
It's rare to meet a deep person, that attempts to understand
Sometimes they are just compelled to stare
Tragedies are compelling and can be foretelling

Does my anguish appeal to the humanitarian in you?
Curiosity? Mockery? People are not all kind
How do you feel about honesty?
I have finally been honest
Eventually living in chains becomes no life at all

Thinking you can keep secrets from yourself is the biggest lie
I try out my new mantra, embrace the pain to break the chains
My paradigm must die
I will write about my struggles
Build character with my hurt
Focus all my energy on my worth

Tear up my obituary, declaring a comeback
Nullify all allegations
Let the wrecking ball of secrets roll
I brace myself for the impact of their **judgments**
My chest rises with a deep breath, I know they cannot help but judge
I cannot help my honesty

IS IT WORTH IT?

Is it worth the cost?
I am wrapping chronic wounds and feeling lost.
My arms are flailing in a graceless place.
Both eyes are searching for a kinder fate.

Preachers should not have families.
Their daughters end up on empty streets.
I am chasing the endless, asphalt stream.
A preacher's kid, looking for a hospital of healing.

I was hurt by what healed you.
Where do I go to be made whole?
I tried turning to the prophets of old.
They do not have a message for me.

Is it worth the cost?
You tell me it is a fight for truth.
Is it also a fight to feel loved too?
I am confused.

You say all these rules are love.
I have faith that I'll know Love's gentle kiss.
I am a child who wants to know the truth of it.
My heart is a mangled puzzle piece--forced to fit.

DIFFERENT ME

I prop up my aching arm with my other
You just continue ignoring me and I bite my lip to keep from crying
I want to remind you that it is your job to be kind
You should not be a teacher if you cannot like kids from different walks of life
Did you know that I can read your mind?
You don't care that I need help or have a question
It is okay
I will figure it out on my own
Just so you can mark my paper with red

You pronounce loudly that I copied and cheated
My face burns red
In front of the class you ask me to pull back my hair and ask me
    probing questions:
"Aren't you cold wearing a dress in winter?"
What do you mean you don't know who that is, don't you have a TV?
It is weird you do not celebrate Christmas or Halloween
Are you in a cult? Do you celebrate anything?"
I do not know
I am just eight

My stomach aches
I can feel you don't like me
I don't know why
It is not for any reason I had the power to decide
I hate being different
It must be so freeing to be all the same
To have someone to play with who does not think you're strange
Access to the spiritual plane is the only thing that makes me feel okay

At lunch I sit alone
I guess I will grow up in poems
Phrases that knit a transformational cocoon
May the world see me when it is my time to bloom
Just hope against hope I feel more accepted with the years
My angel-friend whispers in my ear
That my cage door is unlocked and ajar
The angel suggests I kick it open and run far

WHERE DO I BELONG

The earth has a smell that I do not like
I am a broken crow that has lost its flight
Common. basic. useless.
Another realm rejects me
What am I good for?

I have poured into purpose
Maybe it was not the divine choice
Because I am still so empty
Purpose has not replied
My spirit is a stranger to my body

My body does not emulate my soul
What is so wrong with me, that I have found no one to care but you?
There is no place for me outside your arms
Take me away
Make me an angel

I've tried to weed my garden
Pull the roots of sadness out
Then I see how she lives and hopes for nothing
Because hope without change brings the worst sadness
It makes me tired

The most upsetting thing is not to go unseen
The worst thing is to be seen by eyes
That **regret to have** seen you
Purpose, I call out your name
I cannot remain the same

Grant me access to new realms
Or end this torture
Where do I belong?
I do not believe I am common at the core. basic.useless.
Grant me angel wings

OK WITH IT

I pronounce out loud
I am okay with it
I cannot play pretend
I do not want to be a copy
I do not want to be mediocre
If it means they would want me

Sometimes I try to change my mind
It always means I lie
I hide my family
I hide my past
If they really knew what I believed
The friendship would not last

I am okay with it
I will just stick to the truth
I do not fit in with the church
I do not fit outside of it
Misfit is what fits
I am okay with it

Alone
      A loner
A piece
     A marked sheep
Arresting anxiety...

I am learning to how to be okay with
                             it (me)

NOT LIKE YOU

Perfection is overrated
Who has all this power to define it to a generation?
Who gives it to them?
I see beauty in almost everyone

The way a person might talk, tilt their head
Their honesty and unique intonations
Unrefined, real beauty
Am I the only one attracted to imperfections?

I will not chase perfection
It is something I will not attain
Plastic surgeons will never be too rich
Symmetry and perfection are illusive

Why waste any more of my time crying,
Because I never found happiness
Where there was none to be found?
Someday, I do want to be able to smile at my reflection

I am going to put this magazine away
Lemmings blindly follow a path to destruction
Salmon fight the current all their lives
Are there any examples of a carefree life?

You can be a tumbleweed
Unrooted, not weighed down
But I will be a **deeply rooted** tree
I will let **trending beauty** go

I will let you chase it
Perfection's **comparisons** would torture everything I see
Not like you
I want to make peace with me

Will I be able to shake free, when **illusions of perfection try to** reshape me?
As a rock **bordering the sea**
Forceful waves beating against me
I am strong, but the pressure of **societal** perfection is relentless

ALONE

Stretched out on my belly
My chin propped in my hands
My tears fall on dying grass
How long are they to last?
I cry silently
Wondering what the point of my existence is
I lean against the trunk of the tree
I am the girl no one sees
No one to listen, so much I want to say
My circle is small and suffocating
Cannot discern between night and day
I am always alone
The orange, crimson, and yellow leaves offer lessons to me
As they defy the breeze, and fight to cleave
Everything cycles, there is no stillness in death
One leaf…then two leaves…lose the battle
They twirl and spin
Settle on the ground
I am crying without making a sound
More leaves fall, telling me it is okay to let it go
I cannot force a friendship
Care has to come in a natural flow
Otherwise as fast as they come, they will go
Let my sadness fall under grace
It seems like I will weep forever
Until the last leaf takes its plunge
It dances in the last light of the sun

I marvel at the glows
The skies' vibrant hues
Pink, orange, and fiery red replacing the blues
The sun sets
I turn my back on the brazen sky
The barren branches sway as if to wave goodbye
I wipe my eyes with my shirt
As I head in the direction of home
With heavens' hope that tomorrow
I will not be alone

Confessions of a Preacher's Kid

CANCEL IT

God, cancel every evil prophecy over my life
They look at me with knives
Even though it all seems right
Every part of this is wrong

Their voices are many
Your voice is the One
My future is coded
So it cannot be undone

You reveal Your plan in actions
That seem to not make sense
I cancel their opposing spirit
By the power of the One who owns all

You have no idea that God is my friend
He calls me daughter
Beware of careless offense
God listens to the broken-hearted

You do not know the door of power you have opened
You do not know the power that you spoke in
Only God's divine will, will come to pass
In Jesus' name, I cancel every opposite plan

DECEIVED

You picked me up from school
The hurt of your past made
   you cruel
Your words changed me that day
You told me I was fat compared to
   the other girls

I was wearing a new blue dress
   that day
I felt so pretty
Your words were a knife to the gut
Sharp with disappointment and
   disgust

Until then, I thought I was a
   beautiful child of God
I was **not-at-all** wrong
Then I tried on your words in
   front **of the mirror**

I saw that I was **not-at-all right**
The world looked different--like my
   consciousness had been opened
I began to see the contrasts between
   rich and poor
I was not content with my world
   anymore

After that, kids at school began to
   tease me
I lost my friends
I did not feel worthy of them
They would make fun of me
   at recess

I could feel your rejection
   but I told no one
You fed me disapproval you had
   to give
All the disapproval you had to live
My parents never knew

I will never hurt a child the way you
   did me
I will see them as God's creation
They are at the mercy of another
I will **not leave wounds uncovered**
   I have kept that promise
I have always been kind
So that I would not cause **the pain**
   that was mine

I have asked God to forgive you
He has given me weapons for your
   words
He has made me shine in His time
I am sorry that I reflected the **all the**
hurt
      you held
                  inside   :(

GOT AWAY

You are religious
Played the part
No respect
People objects
Lacking heart

The greedy lose everything
They win for a season
You should listen when we say no
Dig up the seeds
You have sown

The harvest at your feet
Will grow to make you weep
Forced your way
Empty words
Bruises hurt

You will be asked for something
Equal in value to what you took
It might take years
Manifest your fears
Appears you got away

Perfect life
Perfect wife
You forgot
We remember
I hope you repented

I AM DROWNING

Show me how to stop my tears
They do not release the pain
Close my ears to the voices
Telling me to change
Forgive my vanity
For calling you unfair

I cry in desperation that You wrap me in your care
Why did You not equip me with more of the talents needed
To live this life I am stuck in?
Day after day, their opinions tie me down
My cheeks are always wet
I went to the doctor because my eyes are so swollen

The skin is red and itchy from the constant overflow
I do not recognize myself,
But I do not know who I am anyway
There are expectations I will never be able to meet
Will You still listen to my prayers?
Why does it feel so hard to be happy?

I need to stop the conversations with self-pity
You know that I know better
Still I am afraid to speak out the truth, so I write
You letters
If I walk with my head down
Maybe they will take pity

A rejected posture is a sad reflection of You
How do I transform myself, and make it all better?
I have heard so many lies
I am not sure I would recognize truth
I am reaching up to give You my pain
I heard that You help the weak to change

I ask for a strength that only Heaven gives
That will open my eyes to the beauty of the life I live
You promised life more abundantly
Abundance is a foreign word on my lips
The thing that keeps me alive
Is dreaming someday you will create something better than what
IS

NO ONE FORGETS

No one ever
No one ever forgets
The moment their eyes were opened

The first time they met
Genuine evil
The light behind your eyes dimmed forever

You washed but could not get clean
You could not see good
You wondered what life was even intended to be

It was hard to sleep because peace seemed so far
You were a barren landscape--an empty space
Beauty seemed like such a waste

You just felt dead
Dead to anything meaningful
Severed connections between mind, soul, and spirit

You could not go back
Could not erase
No one forgets how evil tastes

THE PROPHET

My body does not want to be fed
My legs will not carry me from
   the bed
I am happier asleep
Floating and wandering another
   dimension

You meet me there in that fleeting
   galaxy
An angelic messenger hands me a
   white dress
My hands run over the
   mulberry silk
I am royalty in it

"Let's put jewels in your hair"
You speak from somewhere
The weight of a crown bears down
   on my head
I square my shoulders, and take a
   deep breath

I know it is all going to be okay
I do not feel heavy in this place
This is a dream, but it is so real
So comfortable here

You see my shut eyes
I feel so relaxed and weightless
Your soft whisper warns, "Do not
   go to sleep.
The prophet is coming"

What will the prophet do?
The angel answers
"He is coming to read what I have
   coded in you

To confirm what you know and
   change what you do"

He spoke to my heart
So the meddling spirits would
   not understand
A leading intuition
That Heaven would touch Earth
   with spiritual plans

My eyes were opened
My mentality changed
For I understood that I am a child
   of God
I am living everything in the
   physical that I am not

When I wake up, how do I make
   them understand?
How do I live who I know that
   I am?
Everything about my life
   must change
Or I will keep wanting to die

I will waste the prophecy in my life
For the prophet called forth a priest
The things he showed me I
   cannot unsee
We are made with the fabric
   of divinity

Confessions of a Preacher's Kid

A FALL FROM GRACE

They told me not to break the rules
I really tried not to
They say evil is an ever-present enemy
Know the principles, know the mistakes
You might never get up if you fall from grace

I stutter: God, I am sorry a million times
You say: My love is long suffering and kind
I say: They want to take my crown away
What is the price You would have me pay?
You say: Stand up straight, and lift your head

I stutter: They say I am taking advantage of Your grace
You say: The price is already paid
My favor is for a lifetime
I say: Do I not have to reap the harvest I have sown?
You say: There are higher laws of grace you do not know

I stutter: You have always blessed me, beyond what I deserve
You have always cared for me, knowing what my sins were
You say: You are my child, and bear my name
I say: Should You not punish me, and make me feel shame?
You say: I know you are sorry; I know you are ashamed

You continue: Pray to me for alignment and strategy
Do not stand in a place of sorrow for too long
The promise of a future will make you strong
I stutter: I am so afraid to face them and declare a new tomorrow
I feel like I owe it to them to suffer with sorrow

You say: Are you theirs or mine?
I am here to help you back into line
I feel a warmth move through me
I remember that Your mercies are new every day
With the rising sun I am fully restored by grace

CHEATER

I thought about myself for way too long
Now I have a life in pieces
My mind is called to the light
I cannot even handle my own truth

My eyes are so dry
They might feel better if I could cry
I cannot speak
Or I would try to fix you with lies

Good thing I have been exposed
It is better to keep silent
When you know you cannot heal
The devastation you have caused

And the doubts he must feel
I am leaving it up to You God
To do whatever You will
You know the depth of my deep

And the fake from the real
I knew that he knew
When I looked in his eyes
I fell to confess from a broken disguise

There is no love like Yours
Your love is so full and so raw
You can heal his wounds
And bring order and law

He does not deserve me
I have proved this a truth
Yet, his love is relentless
Just like You

SAME SAGA

My arms are full of presents to make me glad
Although You send me words of love
I just feel sad
There are precious jewels I hold
But sometimes I just feel worthless
My heart feels old
The way is simple
I have all that I need
It just feels complicated, and I fight unbelief
You knock at my door
Sometimes I still let You in
I might be scared that You will take the thing I love away
What if You make me love the things now that I hate?
I wish I would not have to do these things to be beautiful
If I were stronger
I could give them up
Wishing for the days when Your opinion was enough
Could I be pure
Like I used to
Need none of these things that I am enslaved to
My soul cries for liberation, but my heart is not sure
Truth seems elusive and so obscure
The years ahead are promising
You have blessed me, and will not take it away
I sense You will be there like You were yesterday
Sometimes I worry about where I will be
How do I fix wanting to run from me
Time marches onward
Will You get fed up while I try to figure out my life?
I am just not sure I know which way is right
Just scared to live in a space that is empty
What if I wake up and find that You left me?
You are probably the only reason I am okay
I need to go back
Where I used to pray

DESCENDING

They said I had the key--still looking for the door.
I want to know the King.
Meanwhile I am sinking.
I am descending with the momentum of frustrated desire.
Surely, I am losing the pull to try.
Empty, hollow, hazel eyes
Touch me, I am numb to feeling.

Above my head there is a single piece of light.
It is a solemn, fading twilight.
Father, did I seek you in the heavenly birthplace to bring me to this
    morbid play?
My unsteady feet are one ladder rung away from Hell
Save me from a failed mission.
Why does it seem like my soul is a mismatch for my body?
Please forgive me for constructing disharmony.

I stare at the belt.
I think of all the moments I failed.
My mouth speaks of wonderful things.
But, my thought life is so full of black.
I try to hope but bring in more lack.

The belt slides to the floor barely making a sound.
I am selfish, lost, and unfound.
If I climb up this ladder will you steady me?
Will you send an angel to throw me a buoy in these choppy waters?
God please forgive me and stop this pitiful momentum.

WHAT WE DON'T KNOW

Your voice travels
Your breath unravels
Metaphysical enigmas
Presents wrapped
To journey back
That merge with the spiritual to form an entity
With another place that shares our space
Do not use extreme words that will turn into your curse
Press on in silence
Do not incite your own violence
By wishing on death or speaking of it
Death will remember you when you've forgotten it's name
Fast or slow
To Death it's all the same
Speak Life, Speak Truth
So they will come to you
Seek wisdom
To avoid prisons
Decide you'll win the fight
Secure the enemy's knife
Carve beauty out of stones
That were thrown and missed you
Your voice is significant and the choices you sit in
Affect generations

CHAPTER TWO
SPIRITUAL INTIMACY

YOUR LOVE

Your love
Free of care
A lush grassy hill to roll down
Laughing like a child
It is cool water to wade in
On a hot summer day
Keeps my soul young
Makes me forget to check the mirror
I feel perfect all day
So full of happy
It spills out of my eyes
Can be so overwhelming
I feel dizzy
It opens my eyes
Outside of time
Your love is eternal
Etched in my being
I do not have to use words
It is all-knowing
All-seeing
I close my heart to everything but You
My escape
Your help arrives early
Company stays late
My heartbeat quickens
At Your Name
When you come to me
Your heart beats the same
I will never desert Your presence
There is nowhere to go
You are my island
You are my home

OUR PLACE

There is something about the ocean
I feel Him as soon as my feet hit the sand
He reaches out for me, and I take His hand
Drinking ocean views
Refreshed
Made new
He knows what I love
The mysteries of what water does
It buries
It carries
As the waves ebb and flow
I am healed in my soul
The Heavens are open
All things to hope in
Just before He goes
His light appears in rainbows
A promise He will come again

ONLY YOU

No one knows my every crushed hope and wild dream
No one has shared in the wonder I have seen
But You

No one can take my frustration, and give me peace
No one can use my tears to grow beautiful things
But You

You do wonderful things for me, although I do not always ask
Your promises have proved to last
I know that I can make it through; I know that I can cope

Your presence empowers me to hope
No one can fix my broken focus, and the mistakes I cannot undo
But the grace that is only You

WHO YOU ARE TO ME

You heal all my first hurts
The most painful memories
You touch them with beautiful light

I am naked to You
There are no flaws that I can hide
You lead me to the healing
    balm inside

I am close to You
I am closer to a child
I laugh easy

My fears are quiet
My sobbing is loud
Your chest is my comfort

A fortress, but I break at
    Your touch
Like a perfect sweetness
Never enough

You rescue me with awareness
You make me wise to the wolf
So I cannot be destroyed

I awaited Your words to awaken
    and exist
My life was made eternal
In the Father of all that is

You put a crown on my head full
    of emeralds
You are the King
I was born royal

You are loyalty
I was born loyal
My eyes are full of stars

He smells like the rain
Fresh pines
He is a shelter that keeps me dry

Although I live in a fallen land
One day my consciousness
Will understand

One day I will awaken
In a place He prepared for me
That is too beautiful for my eyes
    now to see

SONG: I WILL WAIT

Chorus
I will wait, I will wait on You Jesus
I will wait, Just wait on You
Until You say it is time
I have made up my mind
To wait, Just wait on You

Verse 1
I begged for life to be easy
Less hurt, Less work
More of the highest successes
But more mess, More stress, Comes up with the sun
I look for a reason
Why I am coming undone
Have I sown
In fields that cannot grow?
Son of God, speak to me

Verse 2
When my next move is planned, it seems
You unplan it
What's planned for me on this planet?
I was born for more, to follow you Lord
I empty myself so I can be filled
Do whatever you need to do
Silence my mind
In the Father I will find
My life's purpose and plan

Chorus
I will wait, I will wait on You Jesus
I will wait, Just wait on You
Until You say it is time
I have made up my mind
To wait, Just wait on You

Bridge
I ask You to be my master planner
Master Planner, let Your hand be on the rest of my life
Even though the sky storms
It ends with beauty

So will Your will be fulfilled in my future
When Jesus moves, He will move mighty in me
Like the night moves for the morning
No mourning, I am renewed
I am purpose, not worthless
You turn the page on my life

SELF WORTH

I got dressed
I looked in the mirror
Took my hair down

I cannot go out like this
Everything is wrong with me
Inside and out

I kicked off my heels
Texted them I was not coming
  after all
Put my face in the pillow and cried

It is better to disappoint them
Let them think I am unreliable
It is better than showing my face

I fell asleep
You called to me
And spoke to my soul

They have taught you all wrong
Being humble is not hating
  yourself
Rejecting your birthright is a sin

I am your mirror
I will tell you what I see
Everything that your being was
  meant to believe

One day you will have it all
I did not make a mistake in who
  I called
I call you a queen

You are salt and light
A lighthouse
You are not meant to hide

Do not deny all the gifts
That are yours to find
You are going to make a difference

I gave you things
Others wish they had
Stop the self-hating and feeling bad

It will cripple you
Take away your power
Let love open you as a flower

So, the next day with swollen eyes
I looked in the mirror
And said, "I love you. You are
God's masterpiece"

YOU TAUGHT ME

It takes so much time
So much endurance to rebuild a level of trust
When a vow has been broken

Selfishness causes ruin
It is not exercising your own will
It is letting yourself be used by powers more powerful than you

Because you refuse to look within
And take a walk with Him
Where God can heal you of infected wounds

It takes more than regretful tears
To redeem time wasted
That God anointed, and He blessed

Repentance is not recounting your sins
Telling God what a bad person you are
Showing Him the pain you have earned

Repentance is not beating yourself up in front of your peers
For a pitiful compassion
Nor begging for a fresh start that will turn out to be a false one

It is letting God see exactly where you are
It is changing your mindset
Your environment and all you have been

Renewing your spirit so you can live
Waking up from a long sleep
To all the wonderful things God says to be

Stop wandering
Be intentional
Meditate on only good

So you can be all that you should
All that God would
Instead of setting fire to bridges, and wasting your life

HOLDING HANDS

My hands tremble with frustration
I do not know what to do
I just want to end it all, but only if I would be with You

Though I sit in darkness,
You are never far from me
Why should God want to show me anything?

Why do I see angels?
No one ever talks about
Why do You send them to work my problems out?

Why are You so good
When You know the reasons why I cry
I do this to myself and let my heart decide

I know You will never leave me
You comfort me when it is all done
You hold me through the lonely hours

You promise me it will get better
It is okay that no one understands
We are of a different world with intertwining hands

All You want from me is for me to leave my hand in Yours
You say You will take me new places
And open realms of doors

MEMORIES

May the good memories live
May the haunting memories die
I ask that God revives those that are meant to survive

God is honesty and can handle our pain
While others run
He helps us change

Time never stops
It keeps on going
It is not stalled by rain, or care if it is snowing

Everything cycles
Seasons go, and seasons come
Regardless of our goals, or what we have done

Whether we like it or not
Time is moving us closer to Him
Turning Heaven's page as the Sun's light grows dim

So many things change
So much stays the same
Locked in number patterns and Time's chain

All I can do with my time
Is be real
I open my heart to God with all it feels

After all, He is my creator
I want Him to be my friend
I want to know God by the time my time ends.

STARTING OVER

Chorus
I'm starting over with Jesus
I'm making a brand-new start
Ready to receive
With open hands
My heart is lifted up
Ready to believe
I'm starting over with Jesus

Verse 1
Please show me mercy and hear my prayer
My heartaches, my troubles are too heavy to bear
I am ready to change
So change me today
I'm ready to give up and do it Your way

Chorus
I'm starting over with Jesus
I'm making a brand-new start
Ready to receive
With open hands
My heart is lifted up
Ready to believe
I'm starting over with Jesus

Verse 2
My sin and my shame, I cannot hide
I know that You see what is inside
I am ready to give up the wrong for what is right
I am ready to surrender and give up the fight

Bridge
Though the tears run like rivers down my face
I'm leaving the altar with new strength
My mind is renewed, I'm not the same
My heart is now free, I feel no more pain

THE ROOM

There is peace in the room where I pray
Your presence
Your essence is waiting
I bend to my knees
Angels entertained
Restoring me
Winds blow from the West
Away with the aging East
My heart is opened
All resistance released
In the room
Anything is possible here
All is found
Affirming sounds
My spiritual eyes see
Contrary things
To the physical realm
The spiritual plane
Miracles are claimed
You show me truth
Expose the lies
I can keep moving forward
Stay in the light
In the room
Overwhelming love
More than enough
A place where Heaven meets Earth
You wait for me
That is amazing
The God that holds the planets and stars
Comes to see the place where His people are

HE UNDERSTANDS

He understands
The wounds that bleed

He understands
The hidden things

He understands
What no person would

He understands
As a father should

He understands
Gives wisdom of old

He understands
Refining gold

He understands
Where my heart really is

He understands
I keep close to Him

He understands
He is my laughter

He understands
Everything that matters

He understands
That is all I need

CHAPTER THREE
BACKSLIDING

BACKSLIDING

Awkwardly backtracking
Lacking answers
Disparaging remarks
Left in the dark
Overstimulated
Complicated
No more
Sick of chores
Passion said goodbye
A long time ago
Ego knows
I must go
Find answers elsewhere
Quiet the mind
Try to unwind
Winding up for a break down
Demas
Haunting lessons
Let the stress in
I am a sinner
Sit in that identity
Does not feel meant-to-be
Fine though
Let perfection go
Overwhelming pressure
Seeking pleasure
Humanity is insanity
Head hurts
So much work
Wish I could walk away
Buy a one-way ticket
Take me far
Lower the bar
Sailing away
No angels of light
Lost fight
Like all the rest
What did you expect
New start
Trying
Backsliding

WHERE IS THE PROMISE?

Why do you live with so little faith?
The blessing is being free to live in the present
Unchained to the past
Unbound to the things that do not last

Your condemnation was carried away in the water
You were reborn to a revelation to call me your Father
You are my child and bear my Name
You have the power to decree change

You walk around in anxiety
Reaching too far ahead
Your vision is broken
The blessing goes unspoken

If you do not live in the present
You will self-destruct
And abort the work
I have chosen for you

I put voices of wisdom in your way
You ignored what the prophets had to say
You wonder where I did you wrong
In not fulfilling my promise

THANK YOU

When I thought You failed me
You told me to wait
You had something better
I was counting on everything I could not see
When I let it go, You came through for me

Thank you for keeping my heart from loving evil
Thank you for teaching me Your ways
So I could live beyond
What my own condemning words
Had power to change

Although chaos lives around me
Attacks all that I sense
You have been my escape
Through trouble, You have shown me
What peace that passes understanding is

I know it has been awhile
Since Your Name has been my lips
Knowing who You are is an overwhelming gift
You have ordered my steps, and aligned my affairs
Thank You for answering forgotten prayers

HAPPY

My vision is blurred
I am so confused
I just feel sick
Used up

I go to church
It all feels wrong
No one loves me there
No friends, and nothing changes

I just let go of all entanglement
All commitment
Pressures of faithfulness
My eyes close

For awhile I feel nothingness
Then I wake up
I do not hear Your voice
Or theirs

Am I free?
Quieted my soul
Turned off my mind
Why do I feel happy?

I can go where the herds go
Live like I have never known
Traded my couture threads
For clothes off the rack

I can drink wine
Forget
Enjoy two-dimensional happiness
And live emptiness

TRUTHS

The words we say
Remove or put obstacles in the way

Our mistakes hurt
At night, they are worse

Forcing obedience
Is oppression

Only the artist knows
The perfect expression and purpose of His work

There is a time to be still and listen
It is hard to listen to understand

I should not live-in frustration and fear
When God is my help and quick to hear

The things we cannot see
Are more real than what we can see

From pain we grow
From experience we can help others

You cannot underestimate love
Love is the perfect law

Self-neglect cripples your purpose
It ensures you will become useless, and help no one

A lie looks so close to the truth
So some people can say self-care is selfish

I must find my own faith
I cannot live off yours

Christians should know the most about words
They could change us and rescue us from religion

God does not want Babylon's castaway materials
Inside God's tabernacle was the best

MISUNDERSTANDING

An Ocean of emotion
Turbulent waves
Bringing change
Not good
But understood
It is my own manifestation

God established the order of the Universe
It's a complex symphony
I fight
All night
A creature of the dark
I delight in fiery sparks

The fruit of our lips is what we get
Not understanding the laws
Insisting we run a democracy with God
Even when we can see
It's a Kingdom
We are taught so little about

So we are unwise
Not knowing the laws
The laws work against us
It isn't what God intended
But we pretend we are okay
Although life does not go our way

Still the law is there
To make our lives go right
The King has his favorites
In the Father, he made us
To be Kings and rule
Exercise our freedom to choose

THEY KNOW I AM A FAKE

I speak louder and louder
It seems I cannot be heard
The more I get
The more I fear
That I cannot be content without it
I cover up how bad that feels

My band-aids are my designer shoes
Can you be friends with your Louis Vuitton?
My confidence is my make-up mirror
Concealer is my magic wand
I fantasize that they think
I have it all

There is a world I am running from
Where I will never be accepted
So I dress myself up to be the best
And more than they expected
God, help me live in quiet peace
So I can have it all

I feel like they can see me naked
In spite of all the pains I have taken
I am scared and hiding
The truth that I am fighting
I should value myself above what I possess
But what do I have apart from the rest?

I was made an artist's muse
But I do not know what I was made to do
I am a fake
Someone tell me imperfect is okay
Can they sense I am living someone else's life?
Show me where I can start living mine

WHO AM I?

Who am I?
I am an eagle
Mostly, I travel alone
Soaring higher

Who am I?
Independent thinker
I draw wisdom from the Word
Strong because I choose to be weaker

Who am I?
Purity is my light
I am elegance
A star made brighter by the night

Who am I?
A loyal friend is rare
I am faithful
Learning from the One who is always there

Who am I?
I am free
Alive in truth
Fresh vision and youth

Who am I?
Never forsaken
Casting all burdens away
Influencer of spiritual change

Do not allow me to forget who I am
An heir
Who almost abandoned it all
Annulled a generational blessing

You kept me
Never left
You helped me answer
The question of who I am

YESTERDAY'S PRAYER

I need your strength
I am not strong
I have quieted my mouth
Surrendered old songs

Give me a new speech
New words
New beauty
Exchanged for ashes

Teach me to hold my peace
I let You have the fight
I have been honest
I have let them be right

I know what it is like to hurt
My hopes and dreams, I divert
Just to please
Always scrambling to appease

I am learning to live without
The thing I never thought that I could
I am learning to do the things
I thought I never would

I will get up
Walk tall
In the face of those
Who watched me fall

I ask for change of pace
Change of place
Where I can be refreshed
And return my best

Victims do not learn from yesterday
The past dictates what they say
I am not trapped in yesterday's prayer
There are no miracles waiting there

MIRROR

When I am not what I should be
Though I sit in darkness
You are never far from me
Why?
Why are you so good?

You know the reason why I cry
You know what I think about all the time
Why are my prayers still answered,
When you see the mistakes I hide?

I look in the mirror
I reproach me
I am nothing like what I should be
I am not pretty

I make cuts in me
You show up and start whispering
Gentle words
Of promise

I know You are the one thing
That will never leave
I do not know why
So I cannot give up on me

You comfort me
When selfishness is done
You tell me fear is broken love
Why do You reach up, and pull out the healing sun?

The day is coming
When my mind will awaken to be free
Gratefulness will return
It will remind my heart of what You did for me

I WISH I NEVER WENT

I do not trust my feelings
Grasping in the water
For something to keep me afloat
There is terrible fate in the depths below

I do not know why I came here
Where is the exit? I need to leave
The trick is leaving behind
Everything seen

I try to dam the confusion
Rushing rivers through my head
Do not let it reach my heart
Before what I left behind
Is ahead

I let go of it
I gave it up a long time ago
I promised Him my hand
I told them all to go

His love is as deep as an ocean
Here, I can only hope to wade
I am sorry that I came
I just want to leave with my hands clean; help me to escape

LONELINESS

Loneliness washes over me
Bathes me with his tears
He is my faithful companion
He whispers to my ear

The things Loneliness says to me
Are shameful to give breath
The words creep into my heart
Introducing death

Loneliness gives my other hand to Sorrow
Sorrow approaches
Asking for some time
She promises to borrow

Depression is bent over by her
Untangling a pile of chains
He is making preparation
For Loneliness and Sorrow to call upon his name

Together they utter satanic prophecies
That God has left me by myself
Alone in this valley I walk through
I am so far away, God could not get to me

I call out God's Name
With a loud and desperate voice
He has never failed to give me joy
Or a reason to rejoice

So, Loneliness wash over me
Bathe me with your fears
I know I am not alone
God is standing near

You are a powerful force
Yet, subject to a Lord
You hover like a storm cloud overhead
I wipe my eyes and repeat what Jesus said

If I resist you
I will be rescued from the many things you are
You cannot overcome me
But watch me worship from afar

My Comforter approaches
Praise pours from my lips
My Consoler wraps His arms around me
I glory in His gift

UNFORTUNATE

I know you think your pretty smile hides
What I can see
In the lines of black mascara that streak your face
Like mud on the streets after it rains

There is an unfortunate maturity
A fortress in your eyes
It breaks my heart
What decision changed your life?

What was sacred
Has been looted
What was private
Is open to the public

You once had a beauty
No one could describe
You once had a glow
That was impossible to find

You only lease yourself now
Someone else owns it
My eyes do not know yours anymore
It is so unfortunate

CHAPTER FOUR
YOU & ME, THINGS FORESEEN

RETROSPECT

It was better to stand alone
Than risk you trying to pull me down
Heartache cured the apathy
You and your friends found

I am here
You are there
Retrospect
Thank God you never cared

Would have never seen the top
If your games had not driven me away
You are stuck inside a box
God equipped me to escape

It was hard to hold myself together
The memories have become my wisdom now
Success has changed my name
The silence taught me how

I will always love you
Cannot help the way I feel
I expect nothing back
My heart is healed

Will you be surprised
To see me in Heaven too
When you lied so much about me
You made-believe the truth

Retrospect told me it would
Everything worked for my good
I was paid treasure for the trial
In retrospect, I smile

A FLEETING PRAYER

He put you in in my path for a reason
He removed you in His season
Sometimes you come to my mind
So I pray
Then you are released
When I say your name
Wherever you are
God's protection is there
He is the One who perpetually cares

LEARNING FAST

You have problems I cannot help you with
So many ugly thoughts inside your head
You tried to give them to me
I chose the positive instead
Tried to tell you what I think
You would not let it in
Let you win
Learned to pace myself
Closed this chapter
Put it on the shelf
I made mistakes
Learned fast
You were a deceptive master class
How was I to know
You were rotten beneath the skin
You preyed upon my innocence
Came from the altar
My knees faltered
Looked fresh
Served regret
I followed advice
I was too naive to fight
You cannot tell
Where the good boys can be found
Until it is too late

MY BEST FRIEND MELISSA

Playing Indians
Old fashioned pioneers
Barefoot in the grass
Dancing over rocks

Laughed for hours
Cut up grass and flowers
Called it potpourri
You understood me

I wish I had been better to you
You were my best friend
My childhood friend
The perfect memories never end

Up all night
Laughing fits
Daring each other to drink salad dressing
Eating all the cookie dough out of the ice cream

You were a dream
A dream of innocence
Nothing bad ever happened to me
With you

A flower
Always smelled sweet
I wonder if you know how much you mean
To me

We could have changed the world
With the energy we shared
A current of joy
Happy intoxicating air

Maybe someday I will see you again
I have changed so much
It would not be the same
But I would love you all the same

WORST THOUGHTS

When I am around you
I have the worst thoughts
I used to think
What in the world?

It is you
Insightful sway
I saw the wolf through the lamb's wool
Witnessed you prey

Knife near her neck
Cooing words
Like sticky sap on your lips
Sucking poison in little sips

Sneaky
So it will not hurt
To get away
With sinister work

Get away
You dark cloud of rain
One day the price will be paid
For the innocent lives you changed

ME

Peonies
Ocean breeze
Pineapple
Apples
Black coffee
Chocolate
Messy hair
Summer flair
Wanting freedom
Dreams
Princesses
Drama
Potential to be
Disney
Actress
Cry easy
The harmony
Lover
Perfect mother
Baker
Faker of happiness
California
Friend of the supernatural
Enjoys dry jokes
Depth that evokes
Learned
Earned
Gym
Win
Love people
Empathy
Empty
Half-Full
Uncool
Beautiful
Eventually seen
All that is me

BREAKING UP

I say that my love for you will be always
Although I had to walk away
Just to make myself feel better
The truth
Love will fade
My heart will change
I will realize through life experience
It was nothing lasting anyway
I am glad we both parted
Despite the years
Despite the tears
It would have cheated us both of real love
You do not know until you know
I trusted to let go
It was the right decision
Not to live in indecision

DEAR FUTURE CHILDREN

I hold you close
Mommy loves you the most
I look at you
I see me
I see my dreams
All that beauty was meant to be

Thoughts consumed with love
My heart is full
Treasures of gold
Your happy dance
Toothy smiles
Serenade my inner child

Everything I never had
Everything that makes you glad
Teach you to be grateful
Teach you to be thankful
Your warmth; I ignore the weather
Every generation does better

Higher successes
Glittering dresses
Country club
Black tux
No Doubts
World Changers you will be

Who am I that God would give me you?
Heaven's art
Brightest stars
Running far
Perfect
Under the surface

I am so in love
Let you grow
Be your own
Trust in God
Uninhibited
My child, your future is unlimited

ADVICE

Off-the-cuff remark
Off-the-record
Should not speak
Will show you are weak

Every action
Met with reaction
Unless you pray
To fall under grace

We make mistakes
Always pay
Unless we change
A positive prayer will get you there

Must address
Have investments
No accidents
Strive to understand it

Invisible is visible
Unseen
Most meaning
Reality is believing

By yourself
Most important time
For integrity
Show the best in me

Gossip
Sticking a knife in yourself
Find something else
To talk about

Do things
Make it seen
Keep your hands busy
It keeps vision alive

Order applies to all things
Even your words
What is heard
Is heard by all

Being critical
Makes you fall
Cannot walk tall
Critical arthritis

Keep your eyes on yourself
No one else
Except to love
Extend an olive branch

Make it right
Wins the fight
Peace at night
I think on only good

There is no transformation in trying
A firm decision redirects the mind
Chasing is keeping it out-of-reach
Desperation is when the soul has overcome the mind to change

LEAVING

I hope you hear Him
I know that He talks
Last we talked about you
As we took a little walk

I know you say you hate me
Hate is frustrated love
I just hope you think about Him
Keep your eyes above

I know you remember
I know you cannot forget
I cannot
But there is nothing He cannot fix

Live your dreams
Do not sell your soul for them
I hope you look for virtues
Let patience be a friend

When you wake up in the morning
Do not feel sad and empty
Let Him love you
His love is more accepting

He thinks that you are beautiful
He thinks your talent is amazing
He will always be there
When the scenery keeps changing

He loves you
I hope you understand
He will be there to hold you
When I take away my hand

HOW YOU TURNED OUT

Time was on your side
You found your stride
I am happy to see you stand
Defiant in foreign lands
Where many failed
The rough seas sailed

A word of faith
Is never late
Insisted on miracles
No one could see
You believed
Abundantly

You looked up to me
To show you free
Now I look up to you
You navigated through
Places I had never been
Experiences I would dream to live

Time proved all things
The fulfillment it brings
Wisdom has completed the work
Proved you a priceless worth
Your birth pulled purpose from my heart
Time made you a work of art

CHAPTER FIVE
CHURCH SPLITS AND OFFENSE

HELP ME TO REMEMBER, HELP ME TO FORGET

Help me to forget
So I can face tomorrow
Help me to remember joy, and forget the sorrow
Help me to remember love, and forget the pain
Help me to forget the loss, and focus on the gain
Help me to forget
Teach me to forgive
Give me strength to go forward and live
Not just exist without happiness
Help me to forget what I saw done
Help me to remember a new day has begun
I ask for your help
Cannot press on within myself
Help me to forget my interminable fears
Help me to forsake the bitter tears
Lift me from this cold, foreboding pit
Help me to remember, help me to forget

TRUTH

Truth
Stagnation
Or transformation
Run away
Or choose to stay
Troubled sighs
As my will dies

Truth
Always causes a reaction
Loose traction
Blood boils
Plans foiled
Not my idea
To submit to Jesus

Only one to give his life
Innocent sacrifice
God in flesh
Different than the rest
Philosophers borrow His truth
Twist and misuse
More than a prophet

We are not God
A part of God
Like God
His DNA
Much the same
Cannot equate
We are not God

Before time began
He was
Made us
At the foundation
Chosen nation
Made spiritual beings

The angels were singing
We need a savior
Within
Without
To abolish doubt
Who created wisdom
That governs universal systems?
Who knows where my soul sleeps?

Wrestle with Truth
The one voice
The one choice
Designer
Refiner
Infallible
I must become malleable

Regardless of personal belief
At His command
Hourglass sand
Stops
We will confess
We are not
God

STRUGGLE

Show me what to do
Give me the power to love them
No matter what they do
They take my freedom away
Help me to love them more each day
Their words are thorns to the heart
Every day, may I restart

Unfair
Do you care?
If You will hold me
I will be okay
Speak through me the words I should say
Let Your love minister through the night
May my silence let You fight

The ones that leave
You give the most
Witnessed by Heaven's hosts
Teach me how to cope
Make me a student of hope
No matter what they put me through
Help me to love them the way You do

I HATE YOU FOR THIS - *My first poem at twelve years old*

All I did was love
It never would have been enough
All you caused was hurt
Seeping, creeping
Into the crevices of my heart
Leaving no untainted parts
You turned what was soft into stone
Broken and alone
I hate you for this

What hurt me the most
Woeful tears that would not stop
Every small and pain-filled drop
Was when you went after the ones I love
The dear ones-- who make my world go round
My family who fills the silence with wonderful sounds
They sacrificed and gave even more than I
You spit when you said goodbye
I hate you for this

I foolishly gave you admiration and respect
You were undeserving
Indifference unnerving
Scars to blame
You feel no shame
I watched them suffer for nothing
For you
Some things you have permanently ruined
I hate you for this

The walls you reduced to rubble
Wish I could escape the trouble
Only if you knew
Or just maybe you do
No more thoughts on you should be wasted
Bitterness I have tasted

I hope you never return
Let the memories burn
I hate you for this

A hot tear slides down my cheek
Comfort I seek
You are my stumbling block
What causes me to struggle
I have even wavered with God
Seeming unable to forgive
For making our lives so difficult to live
Why is it so crippling?
I hate you for this

It can be so hard to put the past behind
There has to be a cure
For all that my parents have endured
Instead of growing easier
It grows harder each day
Why do the righteous have to pay?
Good plans foiled and laughter we've missed
Just to let you know
I hate you for this

SMOTHERING

Smothering
Obsessing
Stressing
Praying
Waiting
Nothing changing
You talk about what is
Not what will be
I do not say anything
Not listening
The tighter that you hold something
The second you release
It will fly as far away as it can get
You cannot smother
Force a lover
Let it go
Set it free
Let it be
Faith is calm
Strong
Sings along
You will get what you worry for
That is sure

GONE

We did not understand the cycle
Although we were learned disciples
Did not know how to stay fresh
Overloaded on stress
We did not focus on the need
Or be everything that we could be
We were tired
We fought
For what did not belong to us anyway
It all belongs to You
We claimed it as ours
Denying envy as it scarred
Ownership robbed us of prophetic words
The vision died and became blurred
So we stuffed our bellies without restraint
We just kept hoping we didn't have to change
Should have affirmed what was ours would come to us
No known strategy of trust
But You could not tell us that
The building disappeared on the evening tide
Suddenly with no goodbye
Pushed to migrate somewhere
Did not know where
Tried to find Your guiding voice
Mulling the choice
No more stars left in the sky
No bosom to rest
To muffle our cry
Full-grown babies
Scared of changing
Afraid of new ideas
We did not know well
Everything cycles
And so **the appointed people** fell

YOU WAITED TOO LONG

We declared
Fasted
Prayed
For your chains
We had the key to fit the lock

You threw rocks
You waited too long

You left
We stayed
You lived your life your way
We lived ours

Eventually a new season came
You waited too long

You knew we always cared
You assumed we would always be there
You felt we were weak in mind
We were kind

When you threw rocks
You waited too long

You were so confused
You knew the truth
Got everything you wanted
Or so you thought

Then you fell on rocks
You waited too long

You thought we were delusional
We were strong
Had been through it all
You had to go through yours

You did not want our help
You waited too long

It was fun and games
Always the same
Until it was not
You really needed us

Then we were gone
You waited too long

CHAPTER SIX
THE ONE

PREPARATION

Teach me
Show me
What real love is
So I can love him
Each day that I live
Take away the desires
Solely my own
Deny the seeds water
That should not be grown
Keep my eye single
My body full of light
A vision of beauty
Starry night
Keep my imagination from evil
My lips the right words to speak
That I may be his strength
If ever he feels weak
You give every perfect gift
A reward for the good we strive to be
I have always believed
That you will be the one
Who gifts him to me

TWO STEPS BACK

Two steps back
A little off-track
The past rebounds
Familiar sounds

Not who I am
Future demands
I be present
In my present blessing

Walls fall
Stack the brick
For back-up
Mixing mortar

It cannot be real
Numb to feel
Want to heal
Wounds that are imaginary

Let go
Demolish walls
Just fall
In love

The past is dead
Peer ahead
You are more than I
Could dream of

Limited mind
God-find
Made for me
In spite of me

In love
So drunk
Stumbling two steps back
Heart attacks

My hand in yours
Is the cure
For everything
You are everything now

Walls fell
I exhaled
One step forward
Into your arms forever

UNBROKEN DREAMS

Glass shatters
Light scatters
Torn seams
I speak of broken dreams
Need peace
Quiet sleep
Time numbs
I succumb to broken dreams
The sun rises
Brings surprises
I can be anyone
Of what broke
I miss-spoke
I cannot lose my destiny
What is mine will come to me
Stain the glass of broken dreams
I claim my stake
In what awaits
In a world of unbroken dreams

WHEN YOU LET IT GO - *To my husband*

Prayed
Every night
Months on end
No friends
Smiled
All the while
Held faith
Things would change
One day
I just let it go

Hours biking
Went hiking
Mountain climbing
Peace of mind
Calm inside
Stormy weather
Whatever
Paper and Pen
Made friends

I had let go
Then you appeared
From nowhere
No clue
It was you
No history
All mystery
Surprised everyone
God laughed

His plan
Not of man
Soul mate
Founded faith
Paths aligned
Treasured find
I knew
It was you
For the rest of my life

THE PERFECT ONE

Higher ways
Cannot understand
I can go the distance
You tell me I can
Alive in Your favor
Surrounded by the blessed
I might be a mistake
But You have chosen me the best
He is the greatest gift
You ever gave
Besides the chance to start reborn
No one could take him
You knew my heart was sworn
A fence of angels
Protects what I love
When I have a request
I pray and it is done
Your miracles enlighten
Passion ignited
Impossible find
I know he is Yours
You made him mine
Higher ways
Praise escapes
For all God has done
Never will I question Your love
In giving me
The perfect One

MY FAVORITE PRAYER

I know my identity
What You intend for me
Is only good
Thank you for renewed mercy
For forgiveness and a renewed mindset
Because You were the spotless Lamb that was slain for the sin of the world
Your blood has been applied to my house through obedience and acknowledging
The great sacrifice of Your Son
I wear Your Name
I am royalty
Because You call me Your child
You have reconciled me
King of Kings
I cast all my burdens on Christ
I walk in total freedom today
I am aware of all my present blessings
Looking ahead
Knowing God's best will continue to manifest in my future
I am God's instrument of peace and love
Because I have sought the Lord to order my steps
I am always in the right place at the right time
Every person I cross paths with today
Has a divine appointment
All opposing spirits
Meddling spirits
Frustrating spirits
Are removed far from my path today
That I may minister in purpose freely
I am open to perceive spiritual instruction
I am healthy and whole
No anxiety
What God intends for me will come at the perfect time
I give thanks for my body
I give it all the attention it deserves
It is a wonderful gift to be alive
My eyes are ready to perceive miracles
My spiritual eyes are open
All things work for my benefit--this is God's promise
I am a blessing to the people around me
It is a blessing to give in abundance
I sow and labor to reap a harvest of good in this life and in the eternal
I declare that through Christ,

> I am blessed, and what
> God has blessed

It cannot be cursed Thank you Father
You are my Sustainer and Protector
In Jesus' Name
      Amen

CHAPTER SEVEN
THE END

HERE TO STAY

Help me do what is right
Stand strong
Walk beside me
The journey is long
Although people leave
Help me to cleave
I know what I am not
I am all that I have sought
Help me not to forget
How You set me free
You extended your arm to save me
An empty vessel
You filled me until I overflowed
Brought me from anonymous to fully known
You taught me that we own nothing
Freeing us from sickness, limitation and disease
Focused on The Source, who called us to dream
If man achieves wealth and fame
At the end of it all
It is all the same--the soul has a need
To return to Father who planted his seed
I have come the conclusion
You are my revelation and guiding truth
There is no life away from You

EPIPHANY

Direct my heart
Rule over my thoughts
Gatekeeper of my soul
Enlighten me with wisdom of old

Then I will overcome
Through the power of the Son
Who holds all knowledge and mysteries
Knowing the origin of time's history

King of all
All power is Yours
Of Heaven and Earth
You weigh my intentions
Called forth my birth

When I see how You see
I manifest impossibilities
Set my sight on the hills
Revealing Heavenly will

In Him all things consist
By Him and through Him
Is all that is made
When I exit the body nothing will change

I have known I am spirit
He is my home
Where I was created
The only place I am whole

BITTERNESS

Heart is ice
Need a fire
He could light
To melt
So I could feel the pain
That belongs to someone else
Compassion
Never lasted
No empathy
Endless seas
Of misery
Harsh judging
Begrudging
Rooted bitterness
Fell over hinderance
Was choice
Now bound
What do I do
I have to love you
Slave to selfishness
My own stubborn ways
Without love I cannot be saved

LOST SHEEP

No understanding of my love
No regard for faithfulness
Still offering grace
Forgiveness
A thief
Who bypassed the Cross
Defend that you are free
Paid no cost
The one door
Ignored
Casual living
Uttering misgivings
Irrepressible pain
Burdening shame
A saintly cry
Pleads for a try
For your hardened heart
Another start
As Jesus did
So you could live
Seasons of mercy
An honored prayer
Dear prodigal son
I will answer their prayer
Intercessors
Intercede
Lost sheep
I appeal to the strong
To hold up the weak

PRICELESS LOVE

My feet become heavier with each step
Rain falls over the miles I wept
I stumble over rocks
Break my fall on thorns
The pain does not compare
To what my heart has borne
My prince
Dressed as a slave
Doing a fool's bidding
Day after day
Anything to reach you
Lessons to teach you
Curse my name
My love remains
The Father calls
The Spirit draws
You poisoned the vines
Mock my kind
I will never interfere with your will
I will close no wounds
Not asked to heal
Time is the enemy
Eternity is at the door
Your death is more important
Than the day you were born
The disciple I sent to tell you the truth
You will meet again in the judgement of you
A crowded road
You have chosen
Passing moments
Not soon enough
You will see
It was a mistake
To forsake
Your royal birthright

WITS END

Deceived
That I achieved
Carnal lusts
Fleeting pleasures
Consequences hurt
Beyond measure
Clever disguise
My demise
Committed apostasy
Intellect involved
No problems solved
Cost me
Misleading wonders
Faith asunder
Seduced with smiles
Gullible child
Bought what you were selling
Believed what you were telling
Intimacy
Sex
Variety
Spicy
Was not enough
Was it?
Instant
Quick visit
Titles
Shiny idols
Money
People love me
Interrupted
Life corrupted
Trapped
Go back
Cannot escape
Fiery lakes
At the end
Of all pretense
I did not know
How this would go
Dear God
Help me

THE LEAST OF THESE

No one saw me coming
Stunning
God was my help
Source of wealth
Chosen vessel
Something special
I have an angel
He guards my back
Anything said against me
He sends an arrow back
I have the best
Because you proclaimed me the worst
He cares about the least
He cares about the deeper things
God will guide you to a solid place
People did not give and they cannot take

ANSWERED PRAYER

God sent an angel to whisper plans in your ear
You heard, although you could not hear
My faith was high
Your faith was on the rise
So you carried out the angelic action
Not knowing that it was a prayerful reaction

The Holy Ghost ministers sending heavenly hosts to work
Men unknowingly obey their whispered words
It is a mystery to us how miracles occur
It all relates to the power of words
God was The Word made flesh
His Spirit releases and arrests

When I truly learned how to pray
I humbled myself bringing His law back to Him every day
I needed answered prayers and He led me to fast
I learned how to put my carnal appetite last
After prayer and fasting, God taught me to tithe and give
When I learned these three, I began to live

SHALOM

     Shalom
A word that lifts your head
Moves you to stand with confidence
     Shalom
Dances like the wind, from The Maker's lips
An ascension to an ether of opulence
     Shalom
Lifts my feet off the ground
Out of Trouble's reach
     Shalom
Peace is sown
Harmony grown
     Shalom
Prosperity makes new
Abundance blooms
     Shalom
Tranquility when times are lean
Wholeness washing the spirit clean
     God, you are my shalom
A source of nourishment for my soul
Shalom is my helper, my place of rest when I go

And when…

I cross over into new provinces

     I will speak a blessing of *SHALOM*

THANK YOU

Dear Reader,

I am so happy to share my journey with you! A journey shared is made easier to bear. Thank you for investing your time and readership in this poetic journal. Please leave a review sharing any impact or introspection this book offered you. It is my prayer you feel the relevance of your own experiences and are inspired to give your story a voice. Take the most care of your own heart.

https://www.facebook.com/Alfiemarchbooks

https://www.instagram.com/authoralfiemarch/

Please e-mail author, Alfie March: prosperitygrapes@gmail.com with proof of purchase for a limited-time gift.

Provide your e-mail/sign up via newsletters for updates, special releases, and journaling resources - https://www.authoralfiemarch.com.

Cover design & layout based on the work by
Ania Halama

Author photograph by
Sara Lockwood

Doodles in L. Edition
By Artist
Olivia O'Toole

Remember: "There is a place that YOU are to fill and no one else can fill something YOU are to do, which no one else can do."
– *Florence Scovel Shinn*

www.ingramcontent.com/pod-product-compliance
Lightning Source LLC
Chambersburg PA
CBHW040424100526
44589CB00022B/2821